AF654689

FROM SHADOWS TO THE SPOTLIGHT

I Believe!

K. Aditya Rao

BookMyStory®

From Shadows To The Spotlight : I Believe!

Published in 2025

© Published by

BookMyStory®

It's time you tell your story

BookMyStory
Thane, 400615, India
info@bookmystorypublishing.com
www.bookmystorypublishing.com

ISBN: 978-93-49509-17-7

About This Book

From Shadows to the Spotlight: I Believe!

There are books that inform.

Books that entertain.

And then there are books that see you.

This is one of those books.

"From Shadows to the Spotlight" isn't just a story of one boy's triumph. It is a gentle but unflinching invitation–to revisit the quiet corners of your own life. The parts you hid. The names you were called. The labels you wore too long. The achievements you chased hoping they'd silence the old wounds.

This book whispers what we all long to hear:

"You're not alone."

"You're not broken."

"You're not too late."

Every Chapter is a mirror. Not to show your reflection, but your *resilience*. You'll find yourself in the TV. In the titles. In the trophy case that didn't fill the void. But you'll also find flight. And fire. And the kind of belief that begins not with confidence, but with honesty.

This is not a manual on success. It's a declaration of significance.

It reminds us that legacy isn't left in LinkedIn updates; it's etched in moments where someone said, "Because of you, I believed again."

Whether you're building a brand, rebuilding a life, or simply searching for your voice—this book won't give you answers.

It will give you yourself.

And that is the beginning of everything.

- K. Aditya Rao

Dedication

To the boy who hid behind the TV.

This book began with you.

With your silence.

With your shame.

With the way you stared at the world, hoping it wouldn't stare back.

You didn't know it then—but every tear, every tremble, every time you shrank inside your skin... was preparing you to speak one day.

And not just speak, but light torches for others still hiding.

To my Father, Dr. Ashutosh Rao

You paused your dreams so I could chase mine.

Your sacrifices were never loud, but they were everywhere.

Thank you for being my first example of quiet courage.

To my Mother, Dr. Jyoti Rao

You are the first fire I ever knew.

Your strength didn't shout–it endured.

You taught me that love is not just felt, it's fought for.

To my Wife and Son, Ranjitha and Ashhvik

You are my why. My wind. My anchor.

In your eyes, I found the reason to become the man I once only pretended to be.

To my Mentors, Dr. Kalim Khan, Dr. Ashwin Malshe, Nitika Didwania and my BNI guides—Hemu Suvarna, Rheet Shroff, Adi Pocha, Nikhil Desai, Morley Patel, Farzana Suri, Bhairavi Mehta, Forum Shah and Aarti Chugani

You didn't just teach.

You challenged me to stop performing and start becoming.

Your belief cracked open doors I didn't even know I had closed.

To my Teacher, Mrs. Lynette Menezes

You saw something in me before I did.

Your trust was the first light I chased.

To my Friend, Namrata Bangera

Your quiet loyalty has been one of the loudest sources of strength in my life.

Thank you for showing up—always.

To Kedar Bhole, who has written the Foreword—an excellent Business Coach/Consultant and Storyteller. Kedar, it's an honor to have you write the foreword. Your contribution has made my book complete.

To the Team and BookMyStory, Rajnish Shirsat and Swapnali Haryan, thank you for relentlessly working behind the scenes to make this book a reality.

And to You, Dear Reader

If you've ever felt unseen, unheard, or unsure of your worth—

This book is your mirror.

Not to reflect who you were told to be—

But to remind you who you truly are.

You are not your wounds.

You are not your labels.

You are the fire beneath your silence.

You are still here.

And that means your story is far from over.

Let's begin.

– K. Aditya Rao

Foreword

There are books that help you think.

There are books that make you feel.

And occasionally, you come across a book that quietly does both and stays with you long after the last page.

From Shadows to the Spotlight is that kind of book.

When Aditya first shared this with me, I expected depth. He's someone I've come to respect deeply not just for his knowledge and branding skills, but for who he is as a person. Calm. Grounded. Thoughtful. Someone who speaks with clarity, listens with intention, and isn't afraid to be vulnerable. There's an honesty in the way he shows up as a coach, a father, a learner and you'll find that same honesty on every page of this book.

This isn't just his story. It's yours. It's mine. It's for anyone who's ever second-guessed themselves, hidden behind labels, or chased shiny objects.

And the beauty is this book doesn't follow a straight line. It's not one of those step-by-step, "do this get that" kind of reads. It flows more l: like a heartfelt conversation—sometimes soft, sometimes intense—filled with moments that make you pause, reflect, and say, "Yeah... I've felt that too."

This book won't give you answers. But it'll give you something far more powerful: perspective. It reminds you that you're not alone, you're not broken, and neither are you too late.

Whether you're rebuilding your life, scaling your business, finding your voice, or just taking a breath before your next chapter, this book meets you where you are.

It's not about becoming someone else.
It's about remembering who you've always been.

Kedar Bhole
Business Consultant | Storytelling Expert | Motivational Speaker

Contents

Chapter 1: The Boy Behind the TV

The Birth of Authenticity

I Believe.

He didn't dream of applause.

He just prayed not to be laughed at again.

He didn't want to win.

He just didn't want to be called fragile—again.

So, he hid. Not metaphorically. Literally.

Behind a television set from the '90s.

Warm. Humming. Box-shaped.

Not because it played cartoons, but because no one looked behind it.

Behind it, he could disappear.

And when you've been stared at your whole life for twitching at the wrong time...

Disappearing feels like mercy.

From Silence to a Spark

I was that boy.

The one with convulsions before he could pronounce the word.

The one who couldn't remember multiplication tables—but could remember how every cousin laughed when he froze during conversations.

The one whose teachers mocked him for his slowness.

The one who crawled under the bed after school because facing his own home felt harder than facing the class.

I wasn't shy.

I was ashamed.

Not just of what my body did—but what it meant to others.

The label: *fragile.*

The subtext: *not enough.*

While my mother—Dr. Jyoti Rao, the physicist with the famed Rangwala- Rao equation to her name—was solving cosmic mysteries...

While my father, Dr Ashutosh Rao, the respected doctor, was tending to lives...

I was just trying to keep mine together.

Medicated for nine years.

Each pill quieted my seizures—and slowly, my spirit.

Your Story Isn't a Liability. It's Your Brand's Foundation.

We think hiding is harmless.

But here's the cost:

When you hide long enough, you start believing you have something to hide.

And that belief?

It doesn't just impact your childhood.

It becomes the root of how you build your brand.

Your business.

Your very self.

Mirror Work: The First Business Plan

Before I ever built my company,

Before I coached founders or spoke on stages—

I stood in front of a mirror...

...and couldn't meet my own eyes.

Because I had titles, yes.

But I didn't have truth.

I was still the boy behind the TV,

Just with better branding.

And here's what I've learned:

You can't build a brand you can't face.

That's why every great brand—personal or professional—starts with the mirror.

The Business Behind Belief

Your audience doesn't just want your product.

They want your presence.

They want your why.

Your pain that became purpose.

Your wounds that became wisdom.

And no, it doesn't make you look weak.

It makes you unforgettable.

Because a brand built on truth

Doesn't just attract customers.

It awakens community.

Tool: Belief Inventory

Take 5 minutes. Ask yourself:

- What core belief still drives my business?

  (e.g., "I must prove I matter.")

- Is it still true... or just familiar?
- Can I rewrite it?

"I was once seen as fragile.

Now, I help others turn their fragility into fortitude."

Your belief becomes your brand.

Your brand becomes your movement.

Business Application: From Hiding to Holding Space

We perform when we want validation.

We position when we choose ourselves.

When I first started coaching, I thought I had to sound smart. Strategic. "Expert."

But that never stuck.

The moment I told the story of hiding behind the TV—

People stopped scrolling.

They leaned in.

Because your clients don't need another expert.

They need someone who's survived what they're still going through.

Worksheet: Craft Your Belief Statement

Step 1: Identify a core wound.

"I was seen as slow and broken."

Step 2: Reframe it as a value.

"I now create spaces where people feel safe to be seen exactly as they are."

Step 3: *Turn it into a tagline.*

"I Believe. Safety isn't silence–it's space."

Personal Story → Core Lesson → Business Strategy

That boy behind the TV?

He didn't vanish.

He evolved.

Every time I take a stage, post a message, coach a client–I think of him.

Because if he could rise, so can you.

That's why your brand matters.

It’s not about showing up perfectly.

It’s about showing up honestly.

Takeaway:

“Your audience doesn’t need another expert. They need someone who’s survived what they’re facing—and can light the way.”

Five-Word Summary:

From silence, a story speaks.

Self-Reflections

- What childhood wound still shapes your business decisions?
- How can your brand serve others who feel unseen?
- What truth are you still hiding behind strategy?

Final Words

You are not a title.

Not a tagline.

Not even your testimonials.

You are the story someone else is waiting to believe in.

You are not behind the TV anymore.

You are the stage.

You are the light.

I Believe.

Chapter 2: Layers & Labels

Shedding to Shine

I Believe.

You don't wake up layered.

You become that way.

Praise the quiet boy? You stop speaking up.

Laugh at the mistake? You aim for perfection.

Mock the pause in your speech? You build a life on performance.

And soon—without meaning to—you've dressed your soul in roles you didn't choose.

I wore mine for years.

- *"Fragile."*
- *"Slow learner."*
- *"The one who needs extra time."*

And later...

- *"The achiever."*
- *"The comeback kid."*

- *"The marketeer who always delivers."*

They looked like growth.

But some were just grief in better packaging.

Because when you're rewarded for overcoming...

You sometimes forget it's okay to just be.

The Trap of Titles

I became the school captain.

Then class rep.

Then the best student in my MBA college.

Then a General Manager.

Then Founder.

But let me be honest—those weren't always choices.

They were shields.

Achievements were applause that drowned out insecurity.

I told myself I was climbing.

But often, I was just hiding better.

Every new label was a new layer.

Every new layer made the mirror harder to face.

Brand Lesson: Outdated Personas Block Real Positioning

You're not the only one.

Businesses do this too.

They wear old branding personas like armour:

- The Always-Available Expert
- The Too-Polished-To-Fail Professional
- The Hyper-Happy Influencer

Each of these begins as a survival instinct.

But over time, they start repelling the very audience we want to attract.

Because people don't buy polish.

They buy presence.

Tool: The Shedding Journal

Start tonight.

Ask:

1. What mask did I wear today?
2. Who was I trying to protect?
3. What truth tried to surface—but I shut it down?

Then write a thank-you note to the mask:

"Thank you for protecting me.

But I don't need you to lead anymore."

My "Shedding" Moment

I was awarded the best marketeer among the best in the business.

And still—I felt like I was disappearing inside.

It wasn't imposter syndrome.

It was *invisible syndrome.*

I was showing up as who I thought the world wanted—

But not as who I was becoming.

Until one day, I stopped writing bios that impressed and started writing truths that resonated.

Like this one:

"I was the boy who once couldn't say 4x6 without stuttering.

Now, I help brands find voices strong enough to lead legacies."

That's not a pitch.

That's a positioning.

Business Check in: The Positioning Check-In

Ask yourself:

- What outdated persona is still running your brand?
- What label are you unconsciously defending with strategy?
- What version of you are you afraid to retire?

Now imagine this:

What would your brand say if it didn't have to impress anyone?

That's the voice your audience is waiting for.

Ritual: Mirror & Message

Every morning, say aloud:

"I release what once served but now suffocates.

I lead not from my labels—but from my light."

Then write one marketing line—from that place of clarity.

You'll notice the difference.

And so will your market.

Personal Branding Isn't Just Telling Your Story.

It's Choosing Which Version to Let Lead.

The "*market-facing*" you isn't supposed to be a mask.

It's supposed to be a mirror.

When I stopped performing strength

and started speaking from the scar—

That's when my brand began breathing.

Practical Tool: Positioning Check-In Template

Label/Layer	Old Role	New Truth
Fragile	Overachiever	I build from belief, not proof
Slow learner	Perfectionist	My pace is not my value
Performer	Always-on Coach	I create from presence, not pressure
"Best marketeer"	Strategy-first professional	I lead with soul and service

This isn't fluff.

This is your new strategy document.

Shedding Isn't Weakness.

It's Brand Evolution.

Just like a snake sheds its skin,

You can shed personas.

Just like a tree sheds leaves,

You can drop what's no longer rooted.

Just like a pearl is formed—

Through layers built from irritation—

Your brand doesn't lose power by peeling back.

It finds clarity.

Takeaway:

"Peel back fear. Reveal purpose."

Five-word summary:

Old labels off. Light leads.

Chapter 3: The Quiet Truth of Belief

From Survival to Significance

I Believe.

Belief isn't fireworks. It's the whisper that says, 'stand up again' when only echoes remain."

---

1. Personal: Healing Through Vulnerability

I carry my mother's equation with me every day.

The Rangwala Rao equation—elegant, precise—balances forces in the universe. Yet no formula could predict the gravity of shame I felt as a child.

When convulsions struck, I learned to split myself in two:

- One half survived the seizures.
- The other half disappeared behind the TV, under beds, inside silence.

For years, I believed my worth was measured by my survival—by staying alive, by hiding effectively.

But true healing began when I discovered the quiet truth:

Vulnerability is not weakness. It's the portal to belonging.

I still remember the afternoon I finally whispered it aloud, to my own reflection:

"I am not defined by what nearly broke me. I am strengthened by what I survived."

My chest tightened. My voice shook. But with that confession, something shifted. The boy who once trembled behind a screen straightened his shoulders—and for the first time, felt the weight lift.

---

2. Core Lesson: Brands That Resonate, Not Perform

Just as an equation needs both sides to balance, your brand needs belief to align every element—from messaging to pricing to client experience.

When you build on performance alone—logos polished, pitches rehearsed—you attract attention. But attention fades.

When you build on belief, you create resonance:

- Emotion over optics.
- Connection over applause.
- Trust over transaction.

Your brand isn't a stage act. It's a heartbeat. It's the rhythm people sync with.

Business Truth:

Brands rooted in vulnerability don't perform.

They resonate.

---

3. Business Application: Story-to-Strategy Map

Transform your pivotal life moments into marketing magic with this five-step map:

Step	Question	Example Answer
1. What happened?	What personal moment reshaped you?	I froze in front of classmates.
2. What belief was born?	What did that moment teach you about yourself?	"If I lose control, I'll lose everyone's respect."
3. What's the truth now?	How have you reframed that belief?	"Showing my scars invites others to own theirs."
4. What's the offer?	How does this truth translate into your service?	A coaching program helping CEOs reclaim confidence through shared stories.
5. What emotion do you evoke?	How do you want clients to feel?	Safe. Seen. Empowered to be unapologetically themselves.

Your memory becomes your message. Your pain becomes your positioning.

4. Tool: Voice Note Ritual

1. Record a 60-second voice note answering:

- "What truth am I most afraid to share publicly?"
- "What part of my story still makes my throat tight?"

2. Listen back—without judgment—three times this week.

3. Notice where your voice softens. Those are the places your audience needs you most.

Why it works:

Hearing your own vulnerability in your voice breaks the illusion of "performance." It reminds you: You are enough—and so is your story.

---

5. Takeaway

"Belief fuels both healing and profit."

---

6. Five-Word Summary

Whispered wounds become resonant brands.

---

7. Self-Reflections

- When was the last time you shared an authentic fear—and it deepened connection?
- What part of your story feels "too real" to market?
- How can you translate that raw truth into your next client offer?

Final Words

Every brand has a secret equation—an invisible formula balancing who you are with why you serve. The only variable that truly matters. Belief.

When you stop surviving your story and start living its lessons, you don't just attract customers—you build a community. You don't just make sales—you spark significance.

You are no longer hiding.

You are no longer performing.

You are resonant.

I Believe.

Chapter 4: The Brand in Your Bones

Legacy Over Likes

I Believe.

Pain doesn't disqualify you.

It brands you.

Not with shame, but with shape.

The kind of shape a soul takes

when it refuses to stay broken.

The boy behind the TV never imagined becoming a business coach.

Never dreamt of keynotes or consultancies.

He only hoped that one day,

people would stop laughing when he walked into the room.

That boy was me.

And the moment I stopped chasing applause,

and started listening to the quiet fire inside—

I began building something that could outlast a like button.

1. Personal: Turning Pain into Purpose

The timeline of my life isn't dotted with milestones–

It's punctuated by heartbreak.

- Ninth grade: My mother was diagnosed with cancer.
- Twelfth standard: Her throat was slit in a brutal attack.
- MBA year: My father–my pillar–suffered a stroke.

And yet...

I became school captain.

A class rep.

An entrepreneur.

A mentor.

A mirror.

Not because I had something to prove–

But because I had something to preserve:

Dignity. Humanity. Meaning.

These weren't motivational moments.

They were mirror moments.

"If everything can be taken from you...

What do you still choose to build?"

That question forged my brand.

Not a logo.

Not a tagline.

Not a funnel.

A decision.

To let the cracks show.

---

2. Core Lesson: Values-Driven Branding

Most brands are built for performance.

Few are built for permanence.

The brands that endure?

They don't chase virality.

They live in values.

Your most painful experiences are not disqualifiers.

They are the proof that you've lived.

And now, you lead.

Tool: Kintsugi Positioning

Kintsugi is the Japanese art of repairing broken pottery with gold.

The cracks aren't hidden–they're honoured.

Try this:

Crack (Wound)	Lesson (Wisdom)	Value (Brand DNA)
Labelled "fragile" as a child	True strength is quiet, enduring	Emotional safety in business coaching
Mother's trauma and recovery	Resilience is born in silence	Compassion and grit in client journeys
Father's stroke during my MBA	Leadership is about presence, not position	Deep empathy in business strategy

The goal isn't perfection.

It's positioning through presence.

---

3. Business Application: The Breath Test

Before publishing, pitching, or posting anything—ask:

- Does this feel like me, or my mask?
- Would I say this if I wasn't trying to impress?
- Is this aligned with who I'm becoming?

If it contracts your chest, rewrite it.

If it softens your shoulders, release it.

Because real positioning shouldn't feel like pressure.

It should feel like a deep breath.

Real-World Strategy: Values Over Vibes

Trends fade. Jargon expires.

But values?

They echo.

Try answering this:

"What truth do I stand on—even when it's inconvenient?"

Now integrate it into:

- Your onboarding documents
- Your sales calls
- Your team briefs
- Your client journeys

Let your values shape your strategy.

Let your scars guide your systems.

---

4. Metaphor: The Clay Cup and the Crack

You are a handmade clay cup.

Maybe you cracked.

Maybe you were shattered.

But you didn't discard yourself.

You rebuilt.

With gold. With grace. With grit.

Now your cracks gleam.

They are the most honest part of your offering.

You are not selling polish.

You are offering presence.

---

5. Positioning from the Soul

When you stop designing a brand to impress strangers–

You start becoming a guide for the ones who need your light.

Brand Truth:

Positioning isn't about finding a market gap.

It's about closing the human gap between your truth and your audience's pain.

Your journey becomes someone else's roadmap.

---

6. Legacy Work: Your Deal-Breakers Define You

List three wounds that shaped you.

Now ask:

- What boundary did that experience teach me to draw?
- What value do I now fiercely protect?
- How can I serve others with that lesson?

You're not just offering a service.

You're offering safety.

And safety is the strongest differentiator in today's business world.

---

7. Takeaway

"Cracks are where your light enters the market."

---

8. Five-Word Summary

Scars shine. Legacy leads now.

---

9. Self-Reflections

- What painful story have you avoided sharing–but deeply defines your brand values?
- How can you turn that story into a safe space for others?
- What does your business look like when built from your bones, not borrowed trends?

Final Words

Your audience doesn't need another guru.

They need a guide.

Someone who's survived what they're still stumbling through.

That someone... is you.

With your golden cracks.

With your whispered strength.

With your brand that breathes like a heartbeat.

You are not broken.

You are branded—by fire, and by faith.

I Believe.

Chapter 5: Boundaries & Burnout

Protecting Your Peace

I Believe.

Success without safety is just survival with better stationery.

There was a time I was applauded by clients, praised by teams, and known in rooms I never thought I'd enter.

And yet—my chest felt tight, my sleep disturbed, my calendar full but my heart completely hollow.

I wasn't overbooked.

I was overexposed.

---

1. Personal: Lessons from Burnout and Self-Betrayal

It's strange, isn't it?

To spend years building a business for freedom—

Only to become its prisoner.

I didn't take calls after 6 because I loved working late.

I took them because I couldn't say no.

Because I feared being forgotten, replaced, or worse—unneeded.

My boundaries blurred into burnout.

And burnout wore a smile.

On the outside?

Peak performance.

Inside?

Peak collapse.

Until one day I looked at my schedule and realized:

"I have built a business that treats me worse than any boss ever did."

That moment wasn't a breakdown.

It was a breakthrough.

---

2. Core Lesson: Lasting brands are built on clear, intentional energy boundaries

We often talk about boundaries like they're fences.

But in branding, they're foundations.

Boundaries are not barriers.

They're blueprints for how you serve and how long you can sustain it.

Every time you say yes from obligation, you leak energy.

And over time, those leaks drown your purpose.

---

3. Business Application: The Alignment Filter

Before saying yes to any opportunity—ask:

- Is this aligned with who I am becoming?
- Am I saying yes out of expansion or fear?
- Would the healed version of me still choose this?

If the answer tightens your gut, it's not your future.

It's your past clinging to relevance.

---

4. Tool: The Emotional Boundary Guide

Not all boundaries are time-based. Some are energetic.

Boundary Type	Example
Time	"I don't take meetings after 6pm."
Emotional	"I don't carry guilt for resting."
Energetic	"My mornings are for creative focus."
Creative	"Not every idea needs execution."
Relational	"I avoid partnerships rooted in ego."

Try this:

Write one boundary for each type this week.

Say it aloud. Then honour it.

---

5. Rewriting the Hustle Narrative

Old Script: "Work harder to prove you matter."

New Script: "Protect your peace. That's your greatest ROI."

Ambition isn't wrong.

But unbound ambition is a form of self-abandonment.

You didn't start your business to escape one boss–

only to become a crueller one to yourself.

6. Ritual: The Weekly Check-In

Every Sunday evening, ask:

- Did I feel resentful anywhere this week?
- Where did I over give, and why?
- What boundary will protect my energy better next time?

Protect your peace like you protect your profit—

Because one cannot exist without the other.

---

7. Takeaway

"Your energy is your equity."

---

8. Five-Word Summary

Protect energy. Grow with grace.

---

9. Self-Reflections

- Where are you betraying your body for your brand?
- What boundaries do you fear setting—and why?
- What does a business that loves you back look like?

Final Words

You don't need more strategy.

You need more sovereignty.

You are not your schedule.

You are not your sales dashboard.

You are the soul this brand was built for.

I Believe.

Chapter 6: Your Story Is Your Strategy

Not What You Sell. Why You Serve.

I Believe.

Once, I hid behind a TV.

Today, I stand on a stage.

And nothing changed—except what I believed about myself.

---

1. Personal Hook: From Disappearing to Defining

That television wasn't just furniture.

It was armour.

It was a sanctuary for the boy who thought his existence was too inconvenient to be seen.

But let's be honest...

Adults don't stop hiding.

We just get more sophisticated.

- We hide behind brand aesthetics.
- Behind "10-step" strategies.

- Behind curated LinkedIn bios and perfect pitch decks.

But if your story is hidden—your strategy will always fall flat.

---

2. Core Lesson: Vulnerability Converts More Than Virality

Your audience doesn't want another expert.

They want someone who's lived what they're living.

Because when your message says,

"I've been there. I believe in you."

It does more than convert.

It connects.

It comforts.

It calls people home to themselves.

---

3. Business Application: The Story → Asset Map

Turn your pain into positioning with this framework:

Story Moment	Asset Created
Hiding behind the TV	Brand Origin Story for website/About Page
Forgetting lines on stage	Keynote opener on shame, fear, and humour
Mother's cancer, father's stroke	Coaching theme on resilience and reinvention
Being called "fragile"	Tagline: "I Believe.™ Fragility is not failure"

This isn't therapy.

It's strategic empathy.

---

4. Worksheet: Craft Your Belief Statement

Step 1: Name the wound

"I was always trying to prove I wasn't broken."

Step 2: Reframe the lesson

"Now I build brands that lead from wholeness, not hustle."

Step 3: Craft the belief

"I Believe. Resilience is the new ROI."

This becomes:

- A keynote theme
- A workshop title
- A brand promise
- A movement

---

5. Reflection Exercise: The Mirror Statement

Stand in front of a mirror and say:

"I am not a brand.

I am a belief.

And today, I choose to be seen—

not for my polish,

but for my presence."

Repeat. Until it feels like yours.

Because it is.

---

6. Takeaway

"Your audience doesn't need another expert. They need someone who's survived what they're facing—and can light the way."

---

7. Five-Word Summary

Story heals. Strategy follows truth.

---

8. Self-Reflections

- What part of your story have you undervalued—but your clients would deeply connect to?
- Where are you performing expertise when your lived experience is enough?
- What pain can you turn into someone else's permission?

Final Words

Your story isn't a soft skill.

It's a strategic asset.

When you lead with truth—your brand doesn't just get attention.

It gets anchored in trust.

You're not here to prove.

You're here to remind.

I Believe.

Chapter 7: Legacy Over Likes

Let Your Brand Echo in Lives, Not Algorithms

I Believe.

You don't need more followers.

You need more echoes.

Let me explain.

One morning, a message landed in my inbox:

"Your story made me walk out of a job I hated for ten years. I cried reading it—not because it was sad, but because it felt like you were talking to me."

There was no CTA.

No funnel.

No likes.

Just legacy.

That message reminded me:

Algorithms expire. But echoes?

Echoes live in lives.

Echoes live in conversations.

Echoes live in courage.

---

1. Personal Hook: A Moment That Mattered

There was a time I obsessed over views.

I'd refresh metrics like I was monitoring my worth.

But one day, after pouring my heart into a talk that barely cracked five hundred views—

A stranger messaged me:

"Because of that one line you said, I called my estranged father."

Five hundred views.

One call.

That's legacy.

---

2. Core Lesson: The Echo Effect

Virality is a flash.

Legacy is a flame.

The Echo Effect is what happens when your brand speaks so deeply...

...it's remembered in therapy sessions,

...quoted in complex decisions,

...felt in car rides home when someone replays your words in their mind.

That's not strategy.

That's significance.

---

3. Business Application: The Legacy Audit

Step 1: Look at your current output.

- *Are you chasing applause or planting meaning?*
- *Are you creating content or conversations that continue when you're not in the room?*

Step 2: Ask:

- *"Who do I want to become a turning point for?"*
- *"How can I serve people before they ever buy from me?"*

4. Tool: The Letter to Your Future Client

Write a letter—not a marketing message, a letter—to someone who hasn't met you yet.

Start like this:

Dear You, Who Feels Invisible...

I've been where you are.

I know the ache of being unseen, unheard, unchosen.

But I also know this:

You are not broken.

You are building.

And this time, you're not doing it alone.

Then sign it not with a pitch—but with a promise.

That's what legacy looks like.

5. Positioning Reflections: Build Campfires, Not Fireworks

Ask:

- Is this launch trying to impress... or create intimacy?
- Is my brand designed to "blow up"? Or to be remembered long after the dust settles?

Build your brand like a campfire.

Quiet. Warm. Gathered around.

The kind of fire people tell stories beside.

---

6. Takeaway

"Likes expire. Legacy endures."

---

7. Five-Word Summary

Echo deep. Forget the feed.

---

8. Self-Reflections

- What's one message your brand must leave behind in others?
- Who would your 10-year-old self be proud you're helping now?
- What kind of story do you want clients to tell after they work with you?

Final Words

You don't need to trend.

You need to transform.

Because the best stories?

They don't just inspire.

They interrupt despair.

I Believe.

Chapter 8: Return to the Mirror

You Are Not Just Seen. You Are the Light.

I Believe.

Let's come full circle.

There once was a boy who hid behind a television.

He believed the world was too loud and he was too broken.

So he shrank.

And the world let him.

But the same mirror that reflected his fear...

One day revealed his fire.

That boy became a man.

That man became a mentor.

That mentor became a mirror for others.

---

1. The Final Mirror

Go to a mirror.

Yes, now.

Stand tall.

Look yourself in the eye.

And say this aloud:

"I survived what I never deserved.

I became what they never saw coming.

I am no longer hiding.

I am the light."

Say it again.

Louder.

Until your bones believe it.

Because this is more than affirmation.

It's activation.

---

2. Final Exercise: Mirror Declaration

Write your own 4-line Declaration of Becoming.

Example:

I was once unseen.

Now, I lead with presence.

I was once afraid.

Now, I am the permission.

Frame it.

Read it daily.

Let it replace the metrics that never knew your name.

---

3. Join the Echo Collective

If this book stirred something in you—

a story, a strategy, a stillness you hadn't allowed—

Then you are already part of the movement.

We're not here for vanity.

We're here for vulnerability that leads to velocity.

We're here for belief.

And for legacy.

You are invited to join the Echo Collective—a space for builders of brave, belief-driven brands.

DM Me on contact@kadityarao.com to know more.

---

4. Closing Line

"The world doesn't need another viral moment.

It needs you—unhidden, unapologetic, and utterly alive.

Now, go build from the light."

Final Five-Word Summary

Be seen. Lead with belief.

Final Reflection

- What truth did this book wake up in you?
- Who will you serve differently because you now see yourself differently?
- What legacy are you willing to begin today, even if no one claps yet?

You are not behind the TV anymore.

You are the torch.

And the world is ready.

I Believe.

Epilogue: This Is Not the End

It's the Invitation.

I Believe.

This book began behind a television.

But it ends in front of a mirror.

Not because the pain disappeared–

But because you showed up.

Not to perform.

But to believe.

You have just read a story that wasn't meant to impress you.

It was written to mirror you.

To remind you that:

- You're not too broken.
- You're not too behind.
- You don't need to be viral to be vital.

You just need to believe.

Let's Recap, Soul First

You learned that authenticity isn't an angle.

It's your anchor.

That the Pearl Method and the Alignment Filter aren't tools.

They're your truth, mapped.

That your brand is not a performance.

It's a presence.

That your childhood wounds didn't delay your destiny.

They defined your message.

That likes are fleeting,

But echoes last.

And that legacy?

It begins the moment you stop hiding.

A Torch, not a Tactic

If you take only one thing from this book, let it be this:

"Your story is not your shame. It's your strategy."

It's not what you sell.

It's why you serve.

Because the people you are meant to serve—

They aren't looking for another expert.

They're looking for you.

Your scars.

Your softness.

Your soul in strategy.

They are waiting to hear a whisper they recognize:

"Because of you... I believed again."

The Echo Collective: A Movement Begins

If this book moved something in you—

a story, a truth, a new direction—

Then you're not alone.

You are one of us.

You are part of the Echo Collective.

We are the brand builders who lead with presence, not pressure.

We speak from scars, not scripts.

We don't chase trends.

We craft transformation.

To the One Still Hiding

If you're still holding back...

Still worried your truth is too heavy, too raw, too real to be part of your brand–

Let me remind you:

I started this journey hidden behind a screen.

Not knowing if I'd ever be worthy of a stage.

But belief doesn't wait for perfection.

It waits for permission.

And that permission?

It begins right here.

With your voice.

With your presence.

With your decision to stop performing and start becoming.

Final Declaration

I am not behind the TV anymore.

I am not my labels.

I am not just seen.

I am the light.

And so are you.

Five-Word Torch-Pass

You're ready. Begin. I Believe.

In the end, I would just like to reiterate...

If this book found its way into your hands at a time when your dreams feel distant and your voice feels small—know this:

you are not alone. We've all stood in that quiet gap between who we are and who we're becoming. This isn't a manual. It's a mirror. And if something stirred within you—an echo, a memory, a buried belief—you've already begun. You don't need a million followers to matter. You don't need a perfect pitch to begin. You just need one thing: someone to believe in you—sometimes that someone is a coach, sometimes it's a reader, and sometimes... it's the version of you that refused to give up. If you're still building in silence, just know—I see you. And I Believe.

About the Author

K. Aditya Rao is a Business Coach, Brand Strategist, and Story Whisperer who helps entrepreneurs scale with purpose, clarity, and heart. With over 19 years of experience across global markets–including India, Vietnam, Indonesia and MENA–Aditya has worked on iconic brands like Parachute, Set Wet, Navratna, Boro Plus and Dove.

He is the founder of Aditya Rao Consultants, and the creator of programs like LaunchLens and Sharpened Brands. Aditya is also a popular visiting faculty member at leading business schools and has coached thousands of professionals and founders across sectors.

His superpower? Helping people rediscover the truth behind their story–and turning that truth into brands that breathe, resonate, and lead.

When he's not writing or coaching, you'll find him being a father, mentor, poet–and the voice behind the whisper:

"You are the light. I Believe."